AF604542
This book belongs to:

This one is for you, little Kimbo Jimbo.
You were right, bugs are cool.—KD

First published in 2024 by
Museums Victoria Publishing
11 Nicholson Street
Carlton, Victoria 3053, Australia
publications@museum.vic.gov.au
www.museumsvictoria.com.au

Many thanks to Dr Ken Walker, senior curator of entomology at Museums Victoria, for consulting on this book.

NATIONAL LIBRARY OF AUSTRALIA
A catalogue record for this book is available from the National Library of Australia

9781921833670 (hbk)

Designer: Julia Donkersley
Production manager: Sasha Beekman

Printed in China by RR Donnelley Asia Printing Solutions, Ltd.

1 3 5 7 9 10 8 6 4 2

Museums Victoria acknowledges the Wurundjeri Woi Wurrung and Boon Wurrung peoples of the eastern Kulin Nations where we work, and First Peoples language groups and communities across Victoria and Australia. Our organisation, in partnership with the First Peoples of Victoria, is working to place First Peoples living cultures and histories at the core of our practice.

This book has been created by Museums Victoria, Australia's largest public museum organisation. Our venues include Melbourne Museum, Scienceworks, Immigration Museum and Royal Exhibition Building. Proceeds from the sale of this book support Museums Victoria's collections and ongoing research.

LUCY LOVES BUGS

Kim Drane

Lucy loves bugs.

Young bugs
and old bugs.

Slow bugs and speedy bugs.

Colourful, glamorous bugs.
Weird and blobby bugs.

Big bugs and
teeny-tiny bugs.

Smooth bugs, bumpy bugs,
spikey bugs, hairy bugs, bugs with
horns and bugs wearing hats.

Definitely the
weird bugs.

You will often find her looking
for bugs in the wild.

Or documenting every single specimen
she can find in her own home.

House fly sleeping on windowsill. Very still. Very hairy.
Beetles. These ones make mum scream! Shiny and really fast.!!
Cheeky little ants helping themselves to a snack!

Sometimes Lucy will collect a bug for further observation ...

... taking extensive notes on their patterns, size, colour and behaviour before returning them home.

But mostly she just watches them
going about their day.

Transfixed by
their teamwork,

their interior
design skills,

and their groovy
dance moves.

Lucy will talk to anyone and
anything about bugs ...

... and she'll talk for
as long as she can.

She has learnt, however ...

... that not everyone shares her enthusiasm for creepy crawlies.

When she's not
talking about bugs,

or drawing bugs,

or looking
at bugs,

Lucy looks at books about bugs.

Lucy has learnt that not all bugs can actually be called 'insects'.

Insects are animals that have:

Two antennae

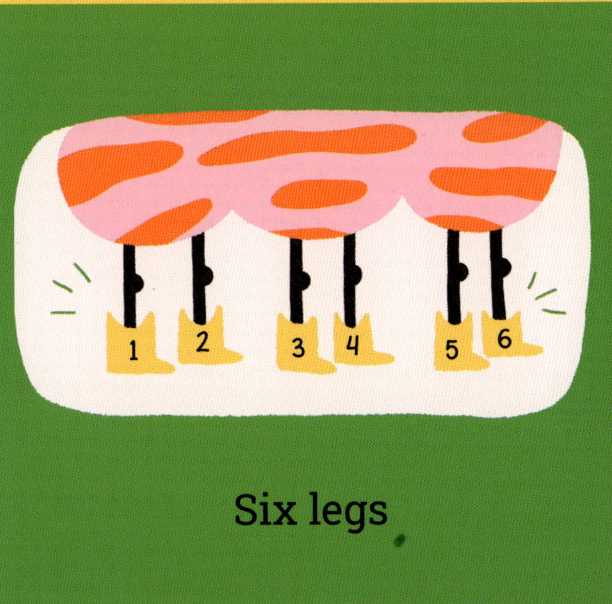

Six legs

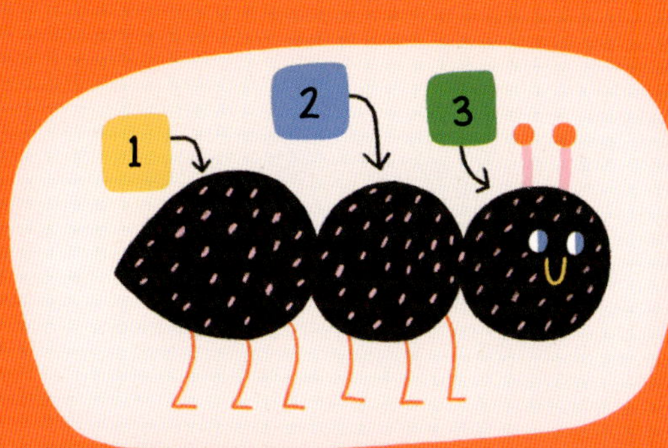

A body made of three parts

A mouth adapted to their unique diet

A skeleton on the outside of their body

Lucy now knows that spiders, worms, substitute teachers and older siblings cannot be scientifically identified as pesky insects.

LUCY

Lucy's dad thinks she could grow up to be a bugologist.

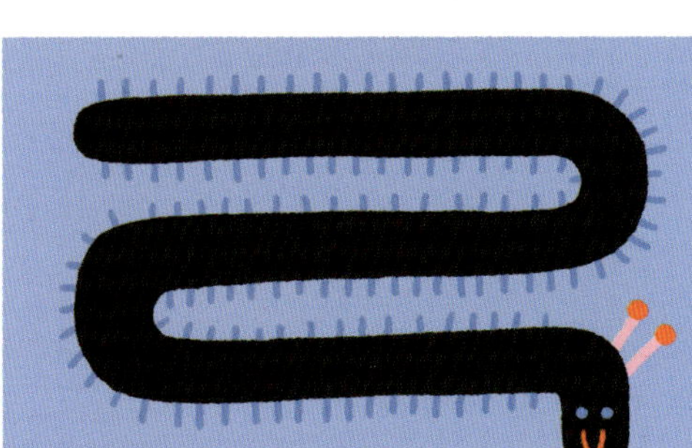

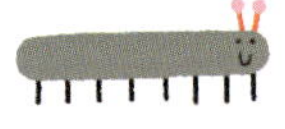

To which Lucy always responds with an indignant, 'It's an *Entomologist!* Not a bugologist!'

But she does agree ...

EN·TOM·OLO·GIST!

She will make a brilliant bugologist one day.

Entomologist (noun):
A scientist who is an expert on insects. 'Entomology' means the study of insects.